Brother, I Love You

because...

★ *A Daily Journal of Gratitude & Love* ★

NICK KEOMAHAVONG

DEDICATION

*This journal is dedicated to all
the siblings who have selflessly provided
support, inspiration, and unconditional
love.*

★ PERSONAL MESSAGE ★

TO:

FROM:

Date:_________________   Day #_______________

I LOVE YOU BECAUSE...

Date:_______________   Day #_______________

I LOVE YOU BECAUSE...

Date:_________________ Day #__________

I LOVE YOU BECAUSE...

Date:_______________________   Day #_______________________

I LOVE YOU BECAUSE...

Date:_______________   Day #_________

I LOVE YOU BECAUSE...

Date:_______________   Day #_____________

I LOVE YOU BECAUSE...

Date:_______________   Day #___________

I LOVE YOU BECAUSE...

Date:_______________   Day #_____________

I LOVE YOU BECAUSE...

Date:_________________________   Day #____________

I LOVE YOU BECAUSE...

Date:_______________________   Day #_______________

I LOVE YOU BECAUSE...

Date:___________________   Day #___________

I LOVE YOU BECAUSE...

Date:_______________   Day #_____________

I LOVE YOU BECAUSE...

Date:_________________   Day #___________

I LOVE YOU BECAUSE...

Date:_____________________ Day #_____________________

I LOVE YOU BECAUSE...

Date:_________________________   Day #_______________

I LOVE YOU BECAUSE...

Date:_______________   Day #_______________

I LOVE YOU BECAUSE...

Date:_________________   Day #_________________

I LOVE YOU BECAUSE...

Date:_________________   Day #_________________

I LOVE YOU BECAUSE...

Date:_________________ Day #_________

I LOVE YOU BECAUSE...

____
____
____
____
____
____
____
____
____
____
____
____
____
____

Date:_______________   Day #_______________

I LOVE YOU BECAUSE...

Date:_________________________ Day #______________

I LOVE YOU BECAUSE...

Date:_______________   Day #_____________

I LOVE YOU BECAUSE...

Date:_________________   Day #_________________

I LOVE YOU BECAUSE...

Date:______________________ Day #________________

I LOVE YOU BECAUSE...

Date:_________________   Day #_____________

I LOVE YOU BECAUSE...

Date:_______________ Day #_____________

I LOVE YOU BECAUSE...

Date:_________________   Day #_________

I LOVE YOU BECAUSE...

Date:___________________   Day #___________________

I LOVE YOU BECAUSE...

Date:_______________   Day #_______________

I LOVE YOU BECAUSE...

Date:____________________   Day #____________________

I LOVE YOU BECAUSE...

Date:_______________   Day #_______________

I LOVE YOU BECAUSE...

Date:__________________   Day #__________________

I LOVE YOU BECAUSE...

Date:______________________   Day #__________

I LOVE YOU BECAUSE...

Date:_________________   Day #_________________

I LOVE YOU BECAUSE...

Date:_______________   Day #______________

I LOVE YOU BECAUSE...

Date:_________________   Day #_____________

I LOVE YOU BECAUSE...

Date:_______________   Day #___________

I LOVE YOU BECAUSE...

Date:_________________   Day #__________

I LOVE YOU BECAUSE...

Date:_________________   Day #_____________

I LOVE YOU BECAUSE...

____

____

____

____

____

____

____

____

____

____

____

____

Date:_________________   Day #___________

I LOVE YOU BECAUSE...

____

____

____

____

____

____

____

____

____

____

____

____

Date:_________________   Day #__________

I LOVE YOU BECAUSE...

Date:_________________   Day #___________________

I LOVE YOU BECAUSE...

Date:________________   Day #__________

I LOVE YOU BECAUSE...

Date:________________   Day #____________

I LOVE YOU BECAUSE...

Date:_________________ Day #__________

I LOVE YOU BECAUSE...

Date:_________________   Day #_________________

I LOVE YOU BECAUSE...

Date:____________ ______   Day #____________

I LOVE YOU BECAUSE...

Date:_____________________   Day #_____________

I LOVE YOU BECAUSE...

Date:_________________   Day #___________

I LOVE YOU BECAUSE...

Date:________________   Day #____________

I LOVE YOU BECAUSE...

Date:_________________ Day #_____________

I LOVE YOU BECAUSE...

Date:_______________________   Day #______________

I LOVE YOU BECAUSE...

Date:_________________   Day #_________________

I LOVE YOU BECAUSE...

Date:_________________   Day #___________

I LOVE YOU BECAUSE...

Date:_________________   Day #_____________

I LOVE YOU BECAUSE...

Date:_______________ Day #___________

I LOVE YOU BECAUSE...

Date:_______________   Day #__________

I LOVE YOU BECAUSE...

Date:_______________   Day #_____________

I LOVE YOU BECAUSE...

Date:_________________ Day #__________

I LOVE YOU BECAUSE...

Date:_______________   Day #_____________

I LOVE YOU BECAUSE...

Date:_______________   Day #___________

I LOVE YOU BECAUSE...

Date:_______________ Day #_____________

I LOVE YOU BECAUSE...

Date:_________________ Day #_____________

I LOVE YOU BECAUSE...

Date:_____________________ Day #_____________________

I LOVE YOU BECAUSE...

Date:________________   Day #___________

I LOVE YOU BECAUSE...

Date:_________________   Day #_________________

I LOVE YOU BECAUSE...

Date:________________   Day #__________

I LOVE YOU BECAUSE...

Date:_______________   Day #___________

I LOVE YOU BECAUSE...

Date:________________   Day #____________

I LOVE YOU BECAUSE...

Date:_______________   Day #___________

I LOVE YOU BECAUSE...

Date:_________________   Day #___________

I LOVE YOU BECAUSE...

Date:__________________   Day #__________________

I LOVE YOU BECAUSE...

Date:_________________   Day #___________

I LOVE YOU BECAUSE...

Date:_______________   Day #_______________

I LOVE YOU BECAUSE...

Date:_________________   Day #_________________

I LOVE YOU BECAUSE...

Date:_______________   Day #__________

I LOVE YOU BECAUSE...

Date:_________________________ Day #______________

I LOVE YOU BECAUSE...

Date:_____________________   Day #_____________

I LOVE YOU BECAUSE...

Date:_______________   Day #_______________

I LOVE YOU BECAUSE...

Date:_________________   Day #_____________

I LOVE YOU BECAUSE...

Date:_______________   Day #_____________

I LOVE YOU BECAUSE...

Date:_________________   Day #_____________

I LOVE YOU BECAUSE...

Date:_________________ Day #___________

I LOVE YOU BECAUSE...

Date:________________   Day #________________

I LOVE YOU BECAUSE...

Date:________________   Day #___________

I LOVE YOU BECAUSE...

Date:___________________   Day #___________________

I LOVE YOU BECAUSE...

Date:_________________   Day #_____________

I LOVE YOU BECAUSE...

Date:_______________   Day #_____________

I LOVE YOU BECAUSE...

Date:_______________   Day #_____________

I LOVE YOU BECAUSE...

Date:______________________   Day #__________

I LOVE YOU BECAUSE...

Date:_________________   Day #_________________

I LOVE YOU BECAUSE...

Date:_________________   Day #_________________

I LOVE YOU BECAUSE...

Date:________________________   Day #___________

I LOVE YOU BECAUSE...

Date:_______________   Day #__________

I LOVE YOU BECAUSE...

Date:_________________   Day #_________________

I LOVE YOU BECAUSE...

Date:________________   Day #____________

I LOVE YOU BECAUSE...